WHAT MATTERS MOST

GRAND RAPIDS, MICHIGAN 49530

ZONDERVAN.COM/
AUTHORTRACKER

www.youthspecialties.com

What Matters Most
Copyright © 2006 by Doug Fields

Youth Specialties products, 300 South Pierce Street, El Cajon, CA 92020, are published by Zondervan, 5300 Patterson Avenue Southeast, Grand Rapids, MI 49530.

ISBN-10: 0-310-27327-7
ISBN-13: 978-0-310-27327-1

Unless otherwise indicated, all Scripture quotations are taken from the *Holy Bible: New International Version*®. NIV®. Copyright © 1973, 1978, 1984 by International Bible Society. Used by permission of Zondervan. All rights reserved.

Web site addresses listed in this book were current at the time of publication. Please contact Youth Specialties via e-mail (YS@YouthSpecialties.com) to report URLs that are no longer operational and provide replacement URLs if available.

Creative Team: Dave Urbanski, Ty Mattson, Laura Gross, Janie Wilkerson, Heather Haggerty, and Mark Novelli
Cover design by Ty Mattson

Printed in the United States
───────────────────────────────

07 08 09 10 11 12 • 10 9 8 7 6 5 4 3 2

Dedication

This book is dedicated to my friend Matt McGill, who has served me faithfully as a coworker and friend for many years and helped me discover *what matters most*.

I also want to dedicate this book to my youth ministry friends (known and unknown) who serve God so faithfully and struggle with pace, balance, and busyness. I know you can win the battle—this book is a friendly letter to "cheer you on"!

Thanks to my friends who read this manuscript and offered me both advice and encouragement. It's so good to have people in my life like you—thanks Duffy Robbins, Marv Penner, Rick Lawrence, Jim Burns, Buddy Owens, Brian Bird, Jeff Brazil, Lance Witt, and Jana Sarti.

I do very few things of worth that my family isn't somehow connected to, and they are the ones who have helped me really see *what matters most*. Cathy, Torie, Cody, and Cassie—you have ignited this message within me to help others discover what I've been looking for. Thanks for living life so well and being so much fun that I can't ever stop thinking about how much I love you.

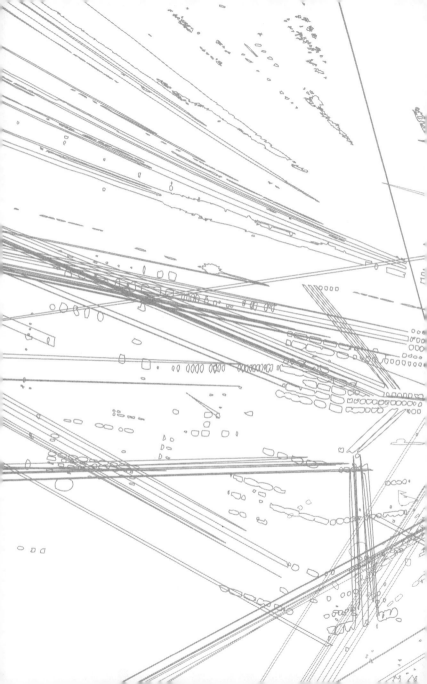

Foreword

Somewhere back in the 20th century I heard Bill Hybels talk to pastors about maintaining a "sustainable pace." I like that phrase. *Sustainable pace*. But a sustainable pace is a lot easier to talk about than maintain. One contributing factor is that few of us know how to read our own gauges. When questioned about our pace, we respond with statements such as, "I can handle it" or "I'm okay" or "This is my busy season."

The problem, of course, is that we can handle it for a while. We *are* okay at the moment, and some seasons are certainly busier than others. Having silenced the voices of concern, we jump back into the current of activity.

To complicate things further, while attempting to sustain an unsustainable pace, we're generally very productive. We have a lot to show for our ceaseless endeavors. Soon we discover that our success creates additional opportunity and responsibility. And since what's rewarded is repeated, the cycle continues.

But all good things must come to an end. After all, an unsustainable pace is—you guessed it—unsustainable. Like an overheated engine, eventually something will break. Odds are it won't be anything related to your ministry. Instead something in your family will break. Perhaps your marriage will break. Maybe your health. Hopefully someone will be there to help you connect the dots, otherwise you'll be tempted to think your problem stems from your ungrateful kids, your uncommitted spouse, or your uncooperative body.

Without some help from the outside, you may be seduced into believing a counselor or doctor can patch things up and get you back in the race before anybody has a chance to lap you.

Not so.

My observation is that the men and women who attempt to maintain an unsustainable pace are rarely aware of it. It could be you. And if so, this might be one of the most important books you ever read.

It may save your ministry. It may save your marriage. It may save your life.

Thanks Doug.

Andy Stanley
North Point Community Church

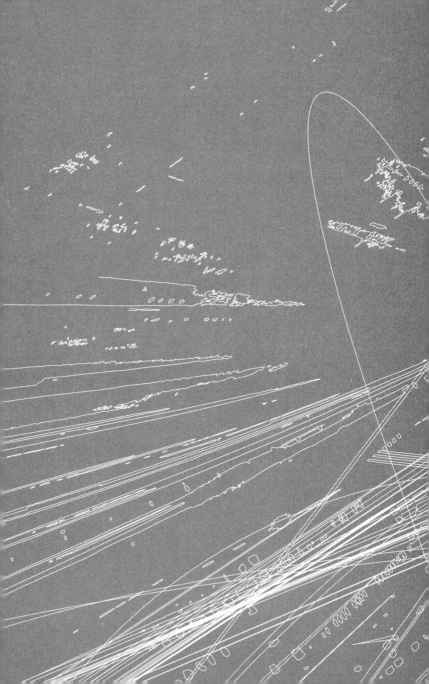

CONTENTS

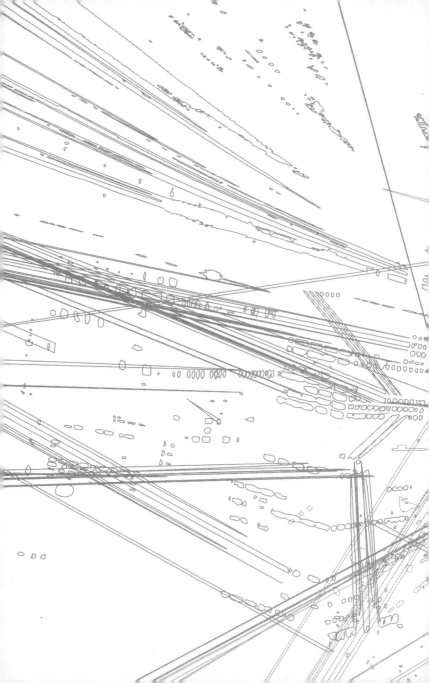

When I started in youth ministry as a volunteer in 1979, I had no idea the pace, the pressure, and the people would demand so much from my personal life.

But as much as I understood God's calling, I was confident God wanted me in ministry. And because others affirmed my calling, I was given leadership responsibility at a young age (mostly because I fit the youth ministry stereotype: young, fun, energetic, and a little crazy).

In the beginning I was confident I could do what I'd observed my youth pastor doing for several years: teaching Bible studies, hanging out with teenagers, eating lots of pizza, and working at a church with a bunch of nice people—all the things that fall under the title of "ministry."

During my early years of youth ministry, I would have never read a book like this! All I cared about were new ideas, fun activities, attractive programs, and ways to increase our youth ministry attendance. I never imagined I would need so much help maintaining a pure heart and staying connected with God. I had so much to learn.

Because in the busyness of my first decade of ministry, I abandoned my first love (God) and developed a love affair with *doing* ministry. I turned into the poster child for doing at the expense of being. I was always busy, always on the move, always armed with new ideas and fresh visions that had to be implemented and conquered immediately. My strong drive and workaholic personality accomplished a lot of ministry, but at the expense of *being* a man after God's own heart.

I was too busy for God—but I figured God would understand because I was busy *for* him.

I had lost something spiritually. I didn't become an atheist—I just sacrificed my intimacy with God for the idols of busyness, achievement, and making people happy. While others were applauding my "success," I was an empty shell in spiritual atrophy.

When I finally admitted my condition to a friend, I realized I wasn't alone. And now, many years later, when I openly talk about the mismanagement of my life and ministry, I realize more youth workers struggle with this than I ever imagined. Not only was I not alone, I wasn't even in the minority! Most Christian leaders can relate to spiritual decay that's a direct result of busyness.

That's why I feel burdened to help youth workers discern *what matters most* in their lives—so they can spend their limited, valuable time focusing on answering that crucial question.

Let me assure you that I'm a very different leader and follower of Christ today than I was in 1979. For starters, no one in my youth ministry considers me young anymore, I'm not as much fun as I used to be, and I don't have the energy I had during my earlier years of ministry. (Pulling an "all-nighter" once meant hanging out all night with teenagers—now it means going to bed without waking up to go to the bathroom.) In other words, I'm definitely not cool (my own teenagers remind me of this daily). But I'm much healthier today—both spiritually and personally.

As someone who genuinely loves youth workers, I write this book hoping you'll be encouraged, challenged, and helped. I've heard plenty of youth workers' horror stories. I've seen firsthand the carnage of damaged ministry lives. I've listened to numerous heart-wrenching accounts of hurting marriages. And I've talked with a lot of good people

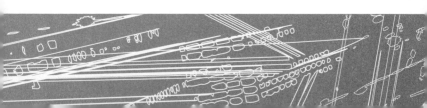

who've given so much of themselves while serving others that their souls are now drained and their spiritual depth is now dangerously shallow.

Whether you're a rookie in ministry or a veteran, if you're not doing the "I've been there" nod in response to what you've read so far, pause long enough to be thankful...and please continue reading and taking notes so you can avoid the personal pain and collateral damage that can happen when ministry leaders don't recognize *what matters most.*

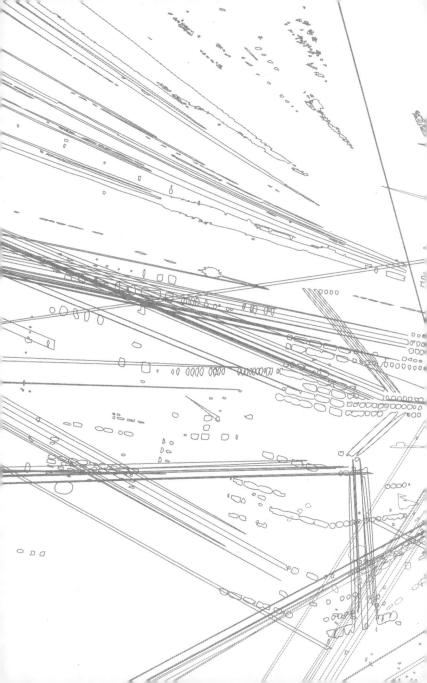

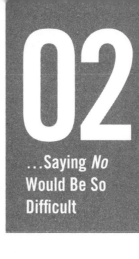

02

...Saying *No*
Would Be So
Difficult

My ministry experiences have taught me a lot about life, God, people, priorities—and me! I've been a youth worker in three different churches (church one for two years; church two for 11 years; and my current church since 1992). Each has been a laboratory to learn ministry, a classroom for education in the ways of people, a sanctuary to investigate and embrace the grace of God, and a woodshed where I've been beaten down and wounded.

Because this is a short book, I'll spare you the details and get right to the most important lesson I've learned.[1] It's summed up with two little words that pack a big punch. You've heard them before: *yes* and *no*. I want to challenge you to say *no* more often so you can say *yes* to *what matters most*.

While saying *no* results in many personal benefits, it's a difficult word for most ministry-minded leaders to utter

[1]For more stories and details about this journey, you might consider reading my book, *Your First Two Years in Youth Ministry* (Youth Specialties/Zondervan, 2002).

because their ministry culture values *yes*. They learn to say *yes* because they want to please others—they don't want to let people down, risk others thinking less of them, or become the target of disappointment or anger.

Does that sound like you? Do you want people to really like you? Do you dwell on it when you learn someone is angry with you? Can you identify with the "logic" that says, "I am a ministry leader, I care about people, and I'm supposed to help others—so when asked, I must figure out a way to say 'yes' at all times"? If so, welcome to my club! Actually I'm trying to cancel my membership, and after many years of fighting, I'm almost out of the club. I think my speech goes something like this: "Hi. I'm Doug, and I'm a ministry-holic addicted to busyness, people-pleasing, saying 'yes,' and the belief that my busyness is a unique season that will soon end." Okay, that's me in pursuit of health and recovery. So I know how difficult it is for you to read this and even consider adding more *no*'s to your responses.

If you're a classic people-pleaser (and we're everywhere in ministry), you'll probably struggle to say *no* more often. You might occasionally say *no*; but when you do, you flinch and lack the confidence or conviction that should accompany a *no*.

If that describes you, please know you're not alone. While *no* is a difficult word to utter, I know you can do it. Actually, I know my fellow youth workers well enough to know that most of them have been longing for the challenge and permission to say *no*. They're at a breaking point and need to take the advice offered in this passage: *This is what the Lord says: "Stand at the crossroads and look; ask for the ancient paths, ask where the good way is, and walk in it, and you will find rest for your souls."* Jeremiah 6:16

You may be at a crossroads in your life and ministry, and the challenge of saying *no* is exactly what you need. So I want to challenge you now: The "good way"

is saying *no*—have the courage to walk in it and find rest for your soul.

Is busyness really getting you what you want—or need? In the end, busyness makes us look important but cripples our relationships. Busyness feeds our egos but ultimately starves our souls. Busyness fills our calendars but fractures our families. And busyness props up our images but shrinks our hearts.

Is there a gnawing sense in your gut that you can't keep up the pace—and in your heart-of-hearts you don't want to? Good! Take a deep breath, and let's go after some hope.

And along the way, here's the principle I want you to get: You need to learn to say *no* to many good things and wonderful people so you'll have space to say *yes* to God, *yes* to the important people in your life, *yes* to priorities—*yes* to *what matters most.*

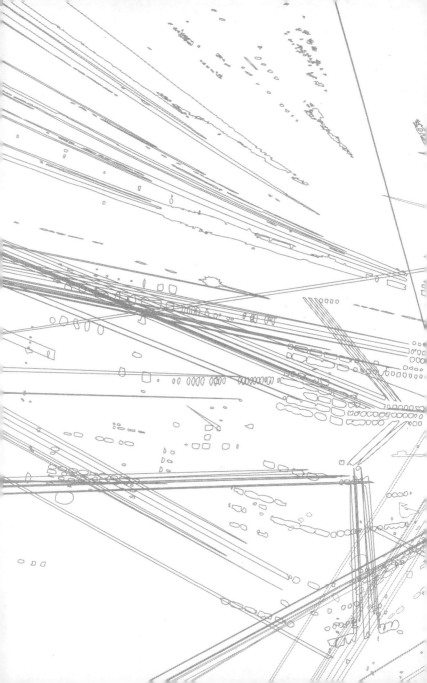

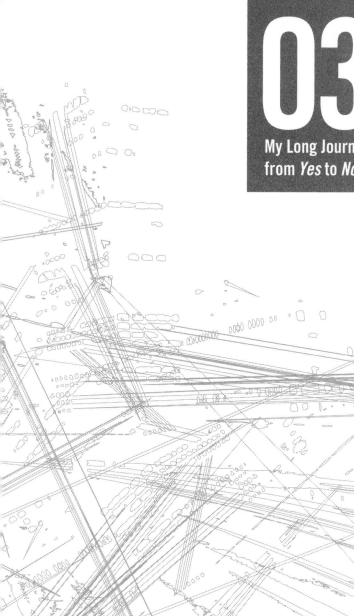

03

My Long Journey from *Yes* to *No*

In all honesty, I felt a little hypocritical when I began writing this book because I haven't completely mastered the art of slowing down by saying *no*. While I'm still on the journey, I'm many years into it; if I waited until I was free of this struggle, I'd never write this book. Actually, knowing what I know about myself, I'm not sure this journey will *ever* end for me. While I walk with more confidence, it's still difficult to say *no* to good things so I can have space to say *yes* to *what matters most.*

Unfortunately, I was years into my ministry journey before I really understood that the busy nature of youth ministry and the craziness of the church culture added octane to my pace. In 1979 I believed the only thing that could be better than being a volunteer youth worker was being a paid youth worker on a church staff. Talk about heaven on earth!

While I was still young and naïve, I honestly believed working in the church would be problem-free and stress-free. I thought people would care enough to ask about my daily time with God. I imagined the water-cooler talk would go something like, "So, who's your favorite disciple?" and "What are you learning in Leviticus?" I anticipated the office bathrooms would contain spare Bibles (with Apocrypha) to enhance my depth while I, umm, paused during my day. And I foolishly believed that as a youth worker I would be well respected and compensated for my dedication to the next generation. I know—young and naïve!

But how could working with Christians all day long possibly be difficult?

Talk about a harsh wake-up call to the reality of working in the church! I quickly discovered that some Christians were mean-spirited. The senior pastor didn't act the same way in the office as he did in the pulpit.

The youth ministry search committee that so kindly interviewed me would prove demon-possessed. People were stressed, unforgiving, and impatient. And my biggest surprise was that everybody seemed to expect me to say *yes* to all of their requests. Plus, I was deeply insecure, wanted everybody to like me, and had my own baggage of frailties that I was bringing into ministry.

What I had idealized as a stroll in the park became a race on the freeway. This ministry culture—filled with overwhelming pressures to perform and please, as well as plenty of resulting heartache—would eventually take its toll on my joy, my spiritual health, and ultimately my ministry effectiveness.

Let's take a closer look at those pressures and heartaches.

PRESSURES THAT FUEL BUSYNESS

I've felt the pressure for more numbers. The church decision-makers made it clear to me that *bigger* was always *better*. Masses were desired over health. *More* was the main value, goal, and gauge for success. Naturally, this pressure to increase also increased my pace.

I've felt the pressure to please everyone. As a young leader I tried to make everyone happy: my pastor, the church administrator, the teenagers, parents of teenagers, my volunteers, and even the church elders. (I soon learned that some elders haven't been pleased with anything since the Eisenhower administration; and though they claimed to have the joy of the Lord, somehow they never informed their faces.) In doing this I convinced myself that the easiest way to please people was to say *yes* to their requests. This pressure to please also increased my pace.

I've felt the pressure to have it all together. Truthfully, I don't believe anyone actually expected perfection, but the church's expressed values didn't seem to allow for failure. So, I'm embarrassed to admit, I pretended to have it all together so people would perceive me as a competent leader. I'd confidently say *yes* to every request every time so others would believe I could accomplish anything asked of me. As you might imagine, this pressure for perfection increased my pace, too.

Like any ministry veteran, I have many personal and painful stories. But I have to state that working in the church has also brought me face-to-face with some wonderful, God-fearing people. I've had a front-row seat to life-change and experiences that I could never adequately describe. To a degree, serving God has been better than my wildest dreams. But it's led to some major heartbreak as well. I've heard mean comments from church leaders, felt nasty manipulations from Chris-

tian parents, and suffered devastating backstabbing by church friends.

How could this happen when my motive was serving God out of obedience to his call? How can this type of pain reside in the church? Easy! The church is made up of sinful people—like you and me—who are capable of doing anything at any given time.

HEARTBREAKS THAT FUEL BUSYNESS

If you're not careful, your heartbreaks can add fuel to your busyness. Heartbreak can also tell you to quit altogether. Or heartbreak can humble you and bring you to a sincere dependence on God and his grace. But most people I know who've experienced heartbreak in ministry ultimately respond by increasing their speed—by doing *more* ministry.

Somehow we believe the lie that if we do "just a little bit more," we can minimize the heartbreak. But please consider how a few heartbreaks might quicken your pace and increase your busyness.

The heartbreak of free will. The theology of free will becomes reality when you see tremendous potential in teenagers who freely choose to live weak and powerless lives. This observation can lead you to believe that if you did "just a little bit more," then you could somehow affect a teenager's free choice. *Result: the pace quickens and busyness increases.*

The heartbreak of critics. In ministry there always seems to be a teenager, a parent, or another church leader who doesn't like how you're doing things. When this happens they usually don't separate *how* you do things from *who* you are. Rarely do they take *you* into account when they speak up, announce your faults, and ultimately crush your spirit. So, in order to

avoid additional criticism, you just work a little harder and do more. *Result: the pace quickens and busyness increases.*

The heartbreak of exhaustion. There's so much to do in youth ministry that you wonder if it will ever slow down. There are too many details, plans, visions, and programs to keep up with. Then, just when you finally feel as though you might be catching up, you hear about another student who slipped through the cracks of your ministry. Sadly, you convince yourself that if you do "just a little more," you can make sure no student ever slips through the cracks again. *Result: the pace quickens and busyness increases.*

The heartbreak of guilt. Guilt appears when you feel as though you don't measure up—to your personal standards or others' unrealistic expectations. The pressure for perfection feels unbearable, and since you're not good enough, you press on to do more and try to

Personal Perspective

- With which of the four heartbreak examples do you most identify?
- If your heart were like the gas tank in your car, how full is it right now?
- What about your other "gauges"? Have you considered your…
- *Spiritual gauge:* Are you practicing Sabbath? Do you study the Bible to feed your soul or to come up with another talk for students?
- *Relational gauge:* Does anybody really know you? Do you have any relationships that go beyond the surface?

CONTINUED >

do it better. *Result: the pace quickens and busyness increases.*

These are just a few of the heartbreaks in a long list that can result in added velocity to your life. You keep doing more and running faster, which means ever-increasing amounts of your heart are sacrificed on the altar of busyness. Your growing to-do list overwhelms your shrinking spiritual life, and you ignore intimacy with God in favor of getting more things done for ministry's sake.

NOT EVERYONE AND EVERYTHING IS MOST IMPORTANT

This truth was the biggest hurdle in my journey toward saying *no* more

often. When everyone and everything is "most important," the response is always *yes*. Unfortunately that *yes* has consequences—among them a busy, chaotic, spiritually dry life.

Something had to give. Someone or someting had to receive a *no.* God had already numbered the hours, minutes, and seconds of my day; he wasn't giving me more time than anyone else. I had to learn that not everyone, nor everything, is most important. I also learned that saying *yes* to more always meant saying *no* to what really *is* most important in my life:

- The tending of my heart
- My spiritual health

- *Family gauge:* Are you always rushed with your kids? How many nights a week are you out doing ministry? If your spouse was asked how connected you are at home, what would be the answer?
- *Personal gauge:* When was the last time you read a book just for the fun of it? What do you do for recreation? What do you do that replenishes your emotions?

- My marriage
- My kids
- My growth
- My personal time

Regardless of your denomination or demographic, you share something in common with everybody else in ministry: A constant *yes*. It's why so many youth workers are tired, lonely, feeling distant from God, and so very busy. Busyness and a consistently enhanced pace can't be maintained over the long haul without some personal and relational damage.

Let me share a story with you.

For about the first month of my marriage, I made the same mistake every night.

I was coming home late for dinner.

Cathy was (and still is) very patient. During our first weeks of marriage she would call me in the afternoon and ask about my arrival time and dinner desires. She was always cheerful and flexible and didn't mandate a time to be home. I was always given the chance to pick the time. Typically I'd say something like, "I'll be home at 6, so why don't we eat at 6:30?"

Things would have gone really well had I arrived home at 6 p.m. like I said I would. Instead, as I was leaving the church office I'd get a phone call from a student who wanted me to drop by his house and see his new drum set. "What a great ministry opportunity!" I'd think to myself, "And it's on the way home..." Or, as I was preparing to leave the office a parent stopped by and asked if I had "just a minute." Or, while packing up to go home I'd realize I forgot to call someone and that it was too important to wait until tomorrow (when I might forget again), so I'd call before I left the office.

Anyway, all these distractions captured my attention, and I was always late coming home. But I really didn't think it was a big deal since Cathy was asking me what time was convenient for me. And it wasn't like I was hours late, just minutes (20, 30, 45 minutes). No big deal because I could justify all the extra time as part of my youth pastor job.

One night while we where having dinner, I politely asked, "Do you mind if I heat this up in the microwave for a minute?" Little did I know that a simple question could lead to tears, screaming, silverware flying, words I hadn't heard her say before (to this day I still believe it may have been tongues), and a quick exit from the table. I thought, "What was *that* all about?"

When I pulled the fork from my neck, it became clear to me that it wasn't about my question; it was about my nightly decisions to make everything and everyone in my youth ministry more important than my bride. I wish I wasn't so stupid then, but I'm thankful that I learned at an early age that some things (ministry add-ons) just aren't as important as other things (my marriage).

So while ministry busyness is often worn as a badge of honor, unfortunately, behind that badge we'll typically find a damaged spiritual life, a damaged family life, and a damaged career. Just because you're busy serving others and serving God doesn't mean you're exempt from the consequences that typically follow an unrelenting lifestyle of busyness.

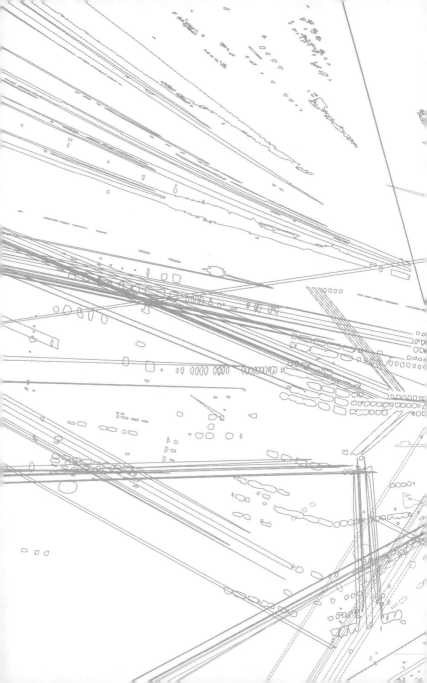

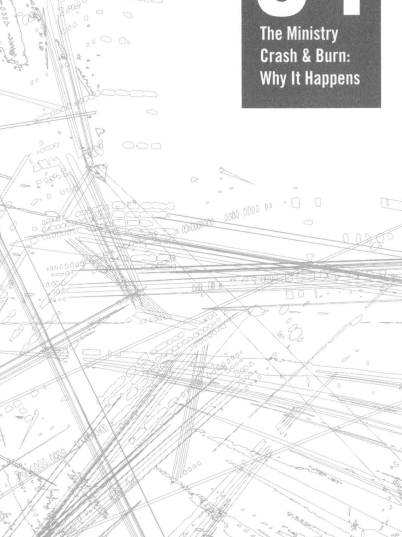

04

**The Ministry
Crash & Burn:
Why It Happens**

Busyness is often the primary factor in a ministry life that crashes and burns. When you're moving too fast, it's difficult to reflect on the past, evaluate your current condition, or focus on the future.

In many ways busyness is like a Chicago train crash that left a lot of damage and injured passengers. The train was traveling almost 70 m.p.h. and had to slow to 10 m.ph., but the conductor didn't pay attention to the warning signs calling for a slower pace. (The Federal Railroad Administration reported that the engineer diverted his attention from safety-critical tasks.) A sad-but-true image of what can happen when you let your life move too fast and disregard the warning signs that indicate a crash is imminent.

Every time you say *yes* to something or someone, you're essentially pushing the gas pedal and increasing the speed of your life. And if you say *yes* frequently, a wreck is likely around the corner. Unfortunately every

time a youth worker crashes and burns, there's a degree of collateral damage, too. Because the church is a body with intertwined parts, others are also affected by your negative consequences. Teenagers, their families, the youth ministry, and the entire church body will feel the pain of one damaged life.

With this particular Chicago train crash, details were released that indicated the crash could have been prevented for at least three reasons:

1) A similar crash had occurred in the same location, which should have led the conductor to take precautionary measures.
2) The warning lights that instructed the conductor to slow down *were* working.
3) The conductor was apparently distracted because he was talking on his cell phone.

Can you see the connection?

We can see these same factors in the lives of men and women who've crashed in ministry:

1) They're not new crashes—someone has crashed that way before.
2) Obvious warnings about the impending crash were ignored.
3) Meaningless distractions led to poor choices.

God has given you the privilege to conduct your own life. You have the freedom to make choices that can lead to God's blessing and favor, as well as painful consequences. While none of us enter ministry believing we'll make bad choices, we often do. These choices aren't made because of our evil hearts, but rather busy hearts that aren't focused on *what matters most*.

I entered youth ministry because I felt as though God called me to serve him by loving teenagers. Honestly, when I started it was all about God and teenagers and loving both with all of my heart. What I quickly learned was that doing ministry with all of my heart meant I was too busy. I can honestly say that during my busyness I didn't intentionally stop loving God and spending time with him, but my passion and love for God was definitely taking a backseat to my passion and love for the church and the activities of the church culture. I can't ever remember making a conscious decision to say *no* to God and *yes* to ministry, but it happened—and unfortunately, it happened a lot. Somehow I took my eyes off of what was most important, and I slowly and unintentionally drifted—a drift that could have led to a serious crash and burn.

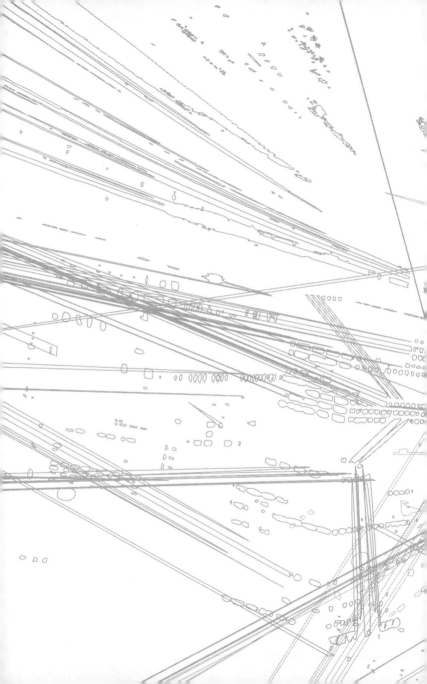

05

Avoiding a Personal Crash & Burn

Please slow down long enough to consider the following questions.

In your current ministry or leadership position—

- Do you want to maintain your current pace?
- Do you take the time to experience and sustain deep levels of relational intimacy with the people most important to you?
- Do you experience the depth of God's love and the closeness he desires when you're too busy to spend time with him?

Many ministry leaders are living their lives at paces that don't allow space for—

- Consistent connections with God,
- Time for the things most critical in your personal life and ministry, and
- Depth with people (you've become a drive-by parent, a run-through spouse, and a text-message friend).

My conversations and observations lead me to believe a high percentage of us ministry leaders need to slow our lives down, learn to say *no*, and take the time to identify *what matters most.*

What matters most to you right now?

- Make a list.
- Then, next to each answer, write a short description of why you believe that particular person or thing deserves a spot on the list of what matters most.
- Sort your list into topics (relationships, personal development, spiritual growth, professional, and so on).

Keep this list in front of you at all times. This visual reminder can help you experience spiritual health, personal depth, and space to really focus on *what matters most.*

Because if you have depth, you will last in youth ministry.

And if you last in youth ministry, you will become more effective.

And if you become more effective, the church will be healthier.

And if the church is healthier, God will be glorified.

Let's face it, there's a lot riding on you defining and experiencing *what matters most.*

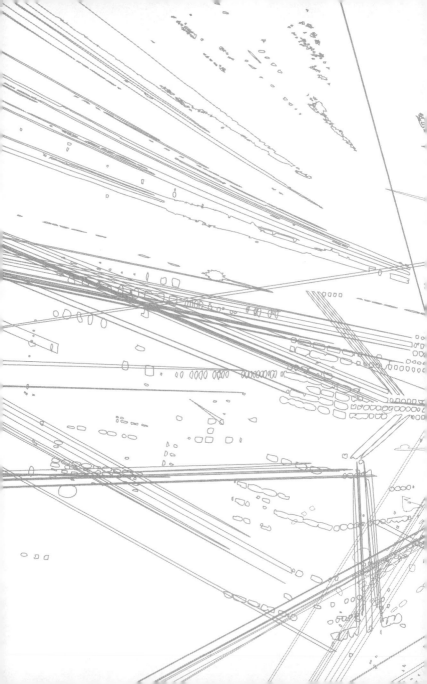

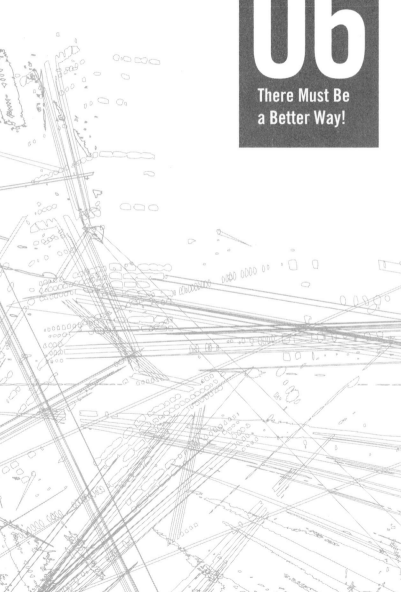

06

There Must Be
a Better Way!

ometimes honesty and reality are ugly, and what you've read so far may grieve your spirit. That's not my intention—but I must warn you that facing these things head-on will not be easy. However, facing them could save your ministry, your health, your family, and your sanity. I want to help guide and coach you toward personal health so you can be more effective for *what matters most*. You don't have to experience the pain and consequences you've just read about. I pray you don't! You can do good youth ministry and be a healthy youth worker without losing your heart, depth, joy, peace, spiritual vitality—or significant relationships. But it's up to you to recognize the warning signs so you know what to say *no* to.

RECOGNIZE THE WARNING SIGNS

Think back to the Chicago train-wreck scenario: Doesn't it seem especially senseless since the warning lights *were* working? They flashed or buzzed and did their

job to warn the conductor, but he was too distracted to notice. Plus, beyond the distraction, the train was traveling so fast that even the conductor's recognition of the warning lights couldn't have slowed it down in time to avoid the crash.

Now think about your own life: Are there warning signs that indicate you're too busy? Do you know when it's time to pull back on the throttle and slow down—or stop? If there are signs, then I have a question: Do you know the warning signs for your own life? Are you observant enough to know when it's time to make some drastic changes so you don't end up another casualty of ministry? If not, you must identify those warning signs that connect to your life.

The following are some warning signs I look for in my life. These may get you started in your own identification process.

Constant clutter. Rushed lives are often reflected in clutter. When I'm too busy, I try to manage my clutter by shoving it into all the closed spaces of my life—filing cabinets, closets, drawers, behind bookcases, under couches—you know the drill. I've come to the conclusion that I don't need a drawer organizer, I need a drawer exorcist.

What about you? Is your desk in need of a makeover? Is it filled with stacks of magazines, letters, lame e-mail illustrations that you printed out to read "someday," seminar notes, pizza boxes (some with a half-eaten pizza still inside), and soon—this book? (Okay, scratch that last one.)

I realize we all have different views on organization and that being messy doesn't necessarily indicate an out-of-control, busy life, but it may be a beginning sign. And it goes way deeper than simply becoming a

neat freak; it's about recognizing that clutter builds up when you're too busy to do anything about it.

Addiction to speed. Obviously I'm referring to the pace of life, not the drug (although taking it might help you get everything done more quickly). This warning sign is evident when you want everyone and everything to move faster. When you're really busy, you tend to talk faster. You even listen faster and nod a lot, hoping the person you're listening to will speed up her speech as well. You may even try to finish her sentences because it may save you some time.

But this desire for everything to go faster follows you to the remote places of your life as well. You want shorter sermons, quick relationships, no waiting, no traffic, not being put on hold, and absolutely no long lines. You identify with the person who walks toward the supermarket checkout stands and computes complex logarithms in an attempt to choose the fastest-moving line: "If I multiply the number of people in line by the number of items in the carts, then divide that number by the age of the checker, I'll identify the fastest-moving line!" Then even after he's made his decision, there's still no peace because he now needs to keep track of where he would've been standing had he chosen a different line. Can you relate?

When you're too busy, it seems as though everyone else is moving too slowly.

Extreme multitasking. You take pride in accomplishing several tasks simultaneously and view yourself as productive and resourceful. You can drive a car, eat, and talk on the phone all at once. Or play video games, watch TV, and prepare your youth sermon all at once. Or clean your hunting rifles while praying for your junior high group. Whatever! You can't focus on one task because you believe every moment must be "maximized."

Superficiality. Busyness is the enemy of depth. It takes time to go deep with others; but if you're too busy, you won't make the time for significant relationships. This communicates that you don't value others and results in relationships that remain on the surface. Your life soon becomes a mile wide and an inch deep. Many ministry people are busy because they're trying to become everything to everyone; instead, they become nothing to no one.

When you don't go deep with others, you'll live in a very shallow place and ultimately become a shallow person. I've watched busy people become so shallow that they don't even understand how their busyness is impacting them.

Relationship fatigue. Busyness robs you of time for significant relationships—family and close friends. This is different from *superficiality* in the sense that you probably already have people in your life to whom you're close and with whom you've previously experienced depth. But now you're too busy to go any deeper. It's not because you don't want to—it's just that you're too tired, drained, and preoccupied to give the best of your presence and love to the people who need and deserve it most. Instead they get cheated and receive your scheduling leftovers—if there are any.

Apathy. Not that long ago there was something about ministry you loved and felt called to. Now it seems overwhelming and impossible. You begin to question if it was God's voice you heard or just minor indigestion. But instead of taking the hard road to figuring it all out, you simply give up. You may still be going through the motions of ministry, but inside you're dry and dying—and instead of taking the hard road to figuring it out, you've started to give up.

Spiritual emptiness. Busyness robs time from God. But you need that time to stay fresh for ministry. I know

some legalistic types who schedule "time with God" on their task list, but it's done more out of obligation than desire. Busyness saps desire.

If you don't have time to slow down, stop, rest, and commune with God—you're too busy!

When you stop to consider that, I'm sure it saddens you. You want connection and intimacy with God, but you just can't seem to find the time to get back on track. I know! You're not alone. Please watch for this warning sign. When you're spiritually empty, your heart for God shrinks. The desire for genuine worship disappears. Compassion for the poor becomes nonexistent. Acts of service that once inspired you now tire you upon consideration. Spiritual malnourishment erodes your soul. You're on the brink of spiritual starvation.

And finally, a word about warning signs: You and I have an amazing ability to self-deceive. We have endless excuses that keep us from recognizing these signs. But others aren't as easily deceived. Are there people in your life who you can ask to spot the warning signs? If so, can you invite them to speak the truth to you?

Personal Perspective

Take a moment to consider the pace of your life.

- Which warning signs can you relate to?
- What can you add to this list?
- What people can recognize these signs in your life? Do they have permission to point them out to you? Why/why not?

RESPOND TO THE WARNING SIGNS

Sadly, even when they recognize the warning signs, many youth ministry leaders don't do anything about them. Maybe we're not sure what to do, or perhaps we don't realize the danger. When you're busy and know you need to change, you actually believe you'll soon slow down long enough to address the issues. I've observed this many times, and the symptoms are surprisingly consistent: apathy, lack of courage to do something, fear of

being found out, and even denial that the warning signs are flashing.

Me? I like to quantify my warning signs with seasonal excuses: "Well, it's just for a short time; I won't be this busy next month." Or "When summer's over, I'll get everything back to normal." These kinds of statements are screams of denial, and I need my close friends to scream back at me (lovingly) and tell me I'm being an idiot.

Here's what most people do when they see the warning signs—nothing. That's right—nothing. But not responding is actually a response. It disguises the real you, allowing everything to appear fine from a distance while your inner life is empty, lonely, and distant from God. Remember: busyness has a price.

DEFINE *WHAT MATTERS MOST*

If you ignore the warning signs that point to busyness, you can be certain a crash is looming in your future. It may not happen this week, this month, or even this year. But it will happen all the same.

Remember: negative character and lifestyle changes are often subtle—almost imperceptible. You don't go from being a committed Christ-follower one day and distant from God the next. And negative actions that accompany busyness usually reveal themselves through poor decisions—choices that trigger a slow, downward descent. Most of the time people don't even see it coming, and eventually they'll say, "I don't know how I became like this."

What about you? Can you see a slow, downward descent in your life? Or have you been hiding so well that you're now fooling yourself, too? This is the point

of the book where you pause and get honest. I beg you to truthfully answer these two vital questions:

1) Do I like the person I've become as a result of my ministry?

2) Is the work I'm doing for God destroying the work of God in me?

Please don't finish this book without giving an honest response to these questions. A truthful answer may create some chaos and pain—that might happen. And as a result of your answers, you may even need to step away from the ministry front lines for a short season. Honesty may require you to give up your lead position for a while in order to renew a right heart for God and others. Your answers may necessitate you telling your boss or supervisor about the condition of your life and asking for accountability and help. I want to be very clear—there may be a cost. But coming clean *before* a crash is far less painful than trying to pick up the pieces *after* the crash.

I've found it quite easy to convince myself of feelings that aren't real: "I'm fine. I'm just a little busy right now, but it'll get back to normal soon." I'm easy to fool. So I try to ask myself these questions on a regular basis, and I'll often share my answers with close friends whom I can't lie to.

I'm also easier on myself when I blame others for my busyness. I find myself thinking that everyone around me needs to change. I reason, "If they'd just change how they do things, it would get better for me." When you read that statement of mine, do you laugh at me or relate to me? Are you also waiting for others to change so you can build more margin into your schedule? If so, let me douse you with a bit of reality I've worn many times:

- Your church isn't going to change.
- The expectations you feel won't go away.

- Your pastor and colleagues aren't going to slow down.
- The pressures of ministry won't diminish.

You must be the one to change! And it starts with saying *no*—or you'll never slow down.

WHY SAYING *NO* IS SO TOUGH

The more I speak with youth workers, the more convinced I am that those of us called to serve others find it very difficult (if not impossible) to say *no* to people and opportunities.

When you reread that, you may protest: "I can say *no* to some things!" Well, of course you can say *no*—to the easy stuff. It's effortless to say *no* to people or opportunities you don't like. If you asked me to volunteer in the church nursery, I'd quickly say, "No." If you offered me an invitation to eat a nasty lima beanvelveeta cheese-cashew-jello salad, first I'd gag; then I'd roll my eyes and say, "No." If you invited me to your house to read the book of Job in Hebrew, I'd say, "Thanks, but no."

What isn't so easy is saying *no* to the many, many good things that come your way in ministry.

Personal Perspective

- Why do I find it so difficult to tell people *no* when I really don't have the time or capacity for them?
- What is it about *no* that bothers me so much?

If you struggle with saying *no* and busyness is affecting you, there isn't an easy way to conquer it. You can't simply slip out of a lifestyle of busyness by making some subtle changes. It won't work! I've tried to do it subtly, but being subtle doesn't communicate the required amount of conviction to do it the right way. I'm not the only one. I know of many others who've

also tried to casually change, but it just doesn't work that way.

To change, you must declare war on busyness—go public, ask for help, and invite others into your journey to change.

Typically, when I evaluate my life in the context of community and talk about the health of my life, it always comes back to how I'm doing too much. And the doing too much results in busyness. I can't tell you how many times I've heard my close friends say, "Doug, you're too busy." When I hear this honest remark from others, I know it's past the time when I needed to change. When others make comments, it's not a warning light—it's a slap upside the head.

But even if you ask others for their opinions, help, and accountability, no one can solve your busyness for you. You must be the one to go into combat mode. It's

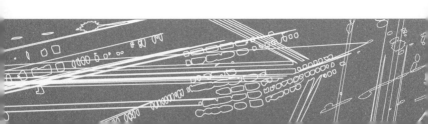

a war! Too much is at stake in your life if you don't take up the battle.

If you want to last in youth ministry...

If you want to go deeper with God...

If you want to have time for your significant relationships...

If you want to live life at a manageable pace...

...then you have to learn to say *no* to more, so you can focus on *what matters most.*

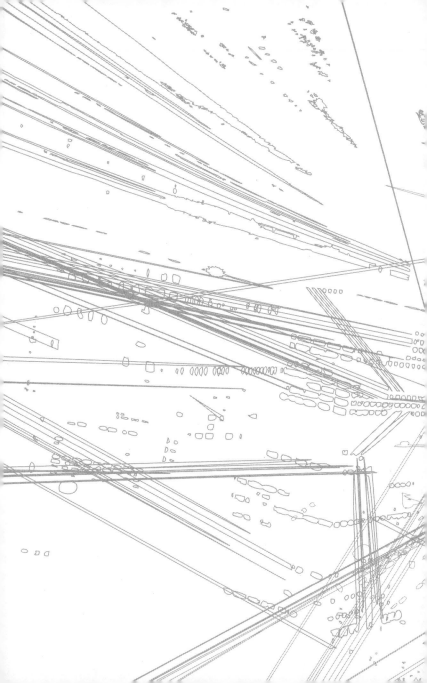

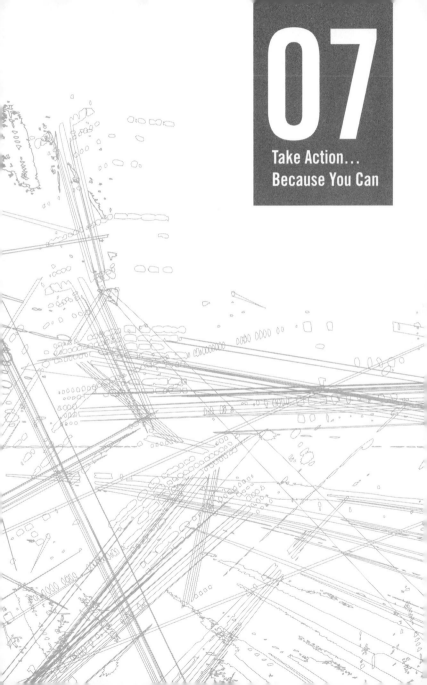

07

**Take Action...
Because You Can**

When I share these ideas with my youth ministry friends, I can read their responses in their eyes: "This all sounds great, Doug. I know I need to slow down. I know I need to say *no*. I know I need to be closer to God. But I don't know where to start." Well, I realize there's no magic prescription that will work for everyone. For me, it's been a long journey of attempts and mistakes. And while I haven't completely arrived, I've taken some strategic actions that have helped me level the playing field and start to believe that I'm turning the corner. Each of these actions involves a key word—*no*—and they're things you can try today. Let's consider them.

SAY *NO* TO MORE NOISE

Most likely you already understand that silence contributes to a more reflective heart and therefore a sloweddown life. Silence is an essential ingredient to a deep spiritual life. Silence is a vehicle for hearing from God.

Elijah didn't hear God in the noise—he heard the *still small voice* of God (1 Kings 19:12, NKJV). God wants to lead us and "speak" to us, but it's hard to hear God through all the noise.

Unfortunately, noise seems to be linked to busyness. And it's not unusual for most people to be around noise all day long. We wake up to noise (alarm clocks) and fall asleep to noise (music or television). When we get into our cars, we typically turn on noise. When we return home, we experience more noise: human noise, media noise, advertising noise, noise about disasters in the news, advice noise, reality-TV noise—so much noise that it forces human noise to become louder in order to be heard. So we try to escape the noise by going for a walk in nature, but we don't want to exercise without listening to some music—more noise. Then we download nature sounds to play at home, hoping they'll help us take a break from all the noise and finally get some rest. It's psycho!

Look for opportunities to turn off the noise. Believe it or not, most noises do have "off" buttons.

Cell phone noise. I often want to ask people, "Are you so critical to the world that you can't turn off your phone during a meal or become temporarily inaccessible while you're at church?" I can't describe how tempted I am to make fun of those who go through their daily lives with their mini-phone strapped to their ear, just waiting to be connected to more noise. It looks very silly, and the word *dork* is always at the tip of my lips when I see it.

Computer noise. Computers are wonderful. I love the one I'm using right now to write this book. But they need to be turned off occasionally. When the computer is on, I feel as though it's calling my name: "Hey Doug! Check your e-mail. You might have something important waiting." E-mail is incessant! E-mail makes me feel as though there's a lurker standing at the front door of my house, and he's knocking obnoxiously

because he knows I'm home. He'll continue to knock until I finally respond. He's screaming, "Yoo hoo! Doug! I know you're there! Answer me. I'm an uninvited intruder expecting you to get back to me right away. Plus, I arrived in your in-box with a red exclamation point—and that means I've cut to the front of the line, and I'm not going away until you respond to me. If you don't answer me immediately, I'll text your cell because I know that's never turned off, either. Where are you? Why haven't you answered me?"

Nonstop e-mail creates busyness because you can never catch up with it.

Media noise. How much time do you spend listening to the radio, the mp3 player, the television, gaming devices, music, podcasts, and so on? Is there ever a day when every waking moment isn't filled with a constant barrage of media noise?

SOLUTION: To learn to say *no* to the noise, you've got to learn two more very important words—*POWER BUT-TON*. I'm not suggesting you reject all technology and join an Amish community, but come on—a less-hurried life requires some silence and reflection. Silence will never come without taking some radical actions such as occasionally turning off, powering down, unplugging, and going off-line.

SAY *NO* TO MORE "SHOW & TELL"

Within the ranks of ministry, there's an illusion of achievement that accompanies busyness. How often do you hear the question, "Are you keeping busy?" The "productive" leader will proudly say, "Yes!" This response is then affirmed with a congratulatory, "Good! I'm happy for you!" This learned cycle of sickness only serves to feed the Yes Monster.

Our insecurities call for a steady supply of achievement-oriented stories at the ready. I call them "Aren't I Wonderful?" show & tell stories. Depending on the depth of our insecurities, we'll either broadcast them (i.e., we're deeply insecure) or hint at them (i.e., we're mildly insecure).

When I attend youth ministry conferences, I'll run into friends from across the globe, many of whom I don't see very often. It's not uncommon for me to ask a simple question such as, "Hey, great to see you! How are you doing?" Then, without hesitation, I'm suddenly bombarded with a show-and-tell achievement story: "The youth group is really growing! The church just went through a major building program where we got to add a great new youth center! I'm writing a new curriculum that I'm hoping to get published, and it's opened up a lot of speaking opportunities for me!"

And this is all stated before I have time to blink. It makes me want to reply, "I asked how *you* are doing, not *what* you are doing."

This is where we need each other's help. We need to stop being impressed by busyness and "achievement." As I mentioned earlier, busyness is a sign of damage, not a sign of honor. When a youth worker is talking about how busy she is, you can be certain something is wrong in her life. Why wrong? God has given us the exact amount of time we need in a given day, week, month, and year. If we're too busy, we're not correctly prioritizing our opportunities or managing the time with which God has entrusted us—therefore something must be wrong.

I'd bet my left arm that the *something wrong* isn't God. And if it's not God, who or what is it? Busyness shouldn't be blamed on God loading your schedule so you have to multitask your way through life. If you're too

busy, and you're resenting sleep as a waste of perfectly good working hours, something is broken with you.

SOLUTION: Instead of valuing a fellow youth worker's activities and achievements, take an interest in the condition of his life. Ask heart questions such as, "How are *you* doing? Tell me about the condition of your inner world." If you're really bold, you might say, "Drop the stories. You don't need to impress me. You're my friend. I care about you. I'd rather know the condition of your soul than how many teenagers you talked to this week and how much you're doing for the youth ministry."

SAY *NO* TO MORE MINISTRY

I really believe that if most youth workers stopped doing half of what they're doing, they'd be spiritually deeper and end up with a healthier ministry to teenagers. Churches would thrive, youth ministries would grow stronger, teenagers and their families would have more time together—and ultimately they'd grow spiritually.

I realize that saying *no* to more ministry is very difficult. I know this all too well because I hate saying *no* to people. But I've been doing it a lot more in recent years; I've come to realize that the healthier I get spiritually, the easier it is to say *no*.

I also realize it's difficult to say *no* because no one wants you to say *no* to them. People can take you on long guilt trips and present convincing reasons why you should say *yes* to them. Have you heard these before?

- "This is ministry—how can you say *no* to an opportunity like this?"
- "Oh, this should only take a few minutes."
- "What would Jesus do?"

Is it possible that Jesus would say *no*?

Jesus said *no* to good things. He said *no* to important people. Jesus often left people unhealed. He didn't

answer every question, go to every event, or meet everyone's needs. He needed time away from his disciples.
He needed space. Yes, he even needed sleep. He was
100 percent God and 100 percent human; therefore,
he had human limits. He needed solitude. He needed
time to reflect and pray and nourish his spiritual life. It
was this life-giving time of connection to the Vine that
gave Jesus spiritual power and energy for his ministry
to others. And I believe it was during those times of
solitude that he was able to hear God's voice and know
what matters most.

Consider how much Jesus had to do. Can you even
fathom the pressure of being the Savior of the world?
He had a short window of time in which to accomplish
his life's mission, yet he seemed to prioritize and live his
life so differently than we do.

To escape others' guilt trips and become more like
Jesus, you'll need to say *no* to more ministry. To say *no*

in ministry is to be radical...and to be counter-cultural...and to be counter-cultural is to be like Jesus...and to be like Jesus is the goal.

SOLUTION: I realize it's easier said (or written) than accomplished—especially if you're paid to minister. You're essentially paid to say *yes* to ministry, right? Yes. Except that if you're getting paid to do ministry, you're also expected—no, *required*—to have depth in order to lead, love, and care for people. Depth requires investment in your inner world. You can't do this when you're always saying *yes* to more ministry.

But I know it's really tough to say *no* to people you love or a request that seems like an easy *yes*. Here's an example that happened while I was working on this book—an e-mail dialogue I had with another pastor at my church:

HI DOUG: On Monday night October 15th, we are having a church membership class. Would you be able to come and speak so we can video you for use in future classes?

HI BRAD: Thanks for asking! Can you please give me another date? Monday is my day off, and I will have just returned from a several-day youth ministry conference where I will have gotten very little sleep. I may actually be dead that day.

DOUG: Don't make me tell you that Pastor Rick is coming in on his day off!!!! Unfortunately, it's the only date we can do it. Come on buddy, please?

(Okay, now watch how I jump off Brad's guilt trip and open up a big can of *no* on him.)

BRAD: If guilt techniques worked on me, I wouldn't have lasted almost 30 years in youth ministry, and I'd probably have a boring job like yours. Let me give you an answer in my bilingual tongue and communicate it in many different languages—"no."

I share this illustration because I want you to know I completely understand how difficult it is to say *no* to conniving, weasel-like, manipulating colleagues-in-Christ who use multiple exclamation points to try to get their way. (Incidentally, Brad's a good friend of mine, and I felt safe using an abrasively humorous *no* with him.)

With that particular request, a *yes* response to teach during that membership class would have become a *no* to several more important things—

- A *yes* would have been a *no* to my Sabbath.
- A *yes* would have been a *no* to rest and reflection.
- A *yes* would have been a *no* to Cathy, Torie, Cody, and Cassie (my wife and kids).

And, quite frankly, being in ministry requires me to say *no* to my family more than enough already. Therefore, when I have the choice, I will say *no* to more ministry so I can say *yes* to *what matters most.*

RECOGNIZE YOU HAVE A CHOICE

The key wording I hope you recognized in the preceding paragraph is, "when I have the choice." Most of the time I really do have the choice to say *no*. Actually I almost always have the choice. Granted, it may *feel* as though I don't have the choice. I may be afraid. I may not like the response to my *no*. I may run the risk of not getting asked again. But I do have the choice. No one holds a gun to my head telling me what choices to make. Busyness is my fault. I'm the one who chose to allow too much in my life.

When I talk to youth workers who relay their perceived no-win scenarios with me, they tell me, "I couldn't say *no*." Usually they say this with such conviction that I almost believe them. But the truth is they really could have said *no* to these requests. They may have had to face negative consequences after saying *no*, but they had to face negative consequences after saying *yes*, too. Remember...someone or something always pays!

That's why it's so important to answer the question, *What matters most?* Your answers will become a helpful filter when you have these kinds of difficult decisions to make.

So when you're facing a tough yes-no decision, and you know there may be a costly consequence, you've got to ask yourself more difficult questions.

Here are the three questions I try to ask:

1) What matters most in this situation?

2) Why do I *really* feel like saying *yes*?

3) What's the worst that could happen if I say *no*?

Let's consider these questions more closely.

1. What matters most in this situation? This is a general question that can immediately help guide an answer. Here's a personal example. One weekend at church, some parents asked me if I would say the prayer at their son's Boy Scout Eagle ceremony on the following Saturday. It was a very nice invitation, and it meant a lot to me that the family wanted me there. I also knew it could be a good ministry opportunity to plant some spiritual seeds in a secular setting and meet some other teenagers who could potentially join our youth ministry. A lot about this invite pointed toward the good.

But I also knew my son had a baseball game at the same time, and I couldn't do both.

I quickly asked myself the question, "What matters most?" The answer: My son. Decision made. Easy! This was a no-brainer. This family may have been disappointed, but I was confident they could find someone else to pray.

My son, however, can't find another dad to attend his game.

If the decisions aren't as easy and clean as this one, then I go to my second question.

2. Why do I *really* feel like saying *yes*? This question allows me to honestly explore my motives. Since I've already admitted having a hard time telling people *no* and usually feel obligated to say *yes*, I need to get at the reasons why.

- Do I want to say *yes* because I'm a classic people-pleaser?

- Am I leaning toward a *yes* because I'm insecure and afraid of the possible response to my *no*?
- Does a *yes* pop into my head because I see this as a way to gain some selfish advancement?

Basically this question helps me uncover my true motives. If my honest answer doesn't reveal a pure motive, then it becomes a lot easier to say *no*. Why would I want to say *yes* for impure motives? That's not a sign of godliness or a mark of integrity.

For me, when I push the "pause" button on busyness and really evaluate my motives for why I feel like saying *yes*, it usually comes back to my insecurities. If I'm honest I have to admit that I live with a desperate desire to be loved, valued, and accepted. And when I say *yes* to others, I usually feel loved, valued, and accepted. My insecurities fuel activity in my life because activity typically results in a form of love, value, and acceptance. If I can admit this motive (and it's painful to do), I can usually stop the activity by saying *no*. When my motive is to say *yes* for human love, value, or acceptance, I try to say this type of prayer: "God, I want to say *yes* only because I want to feel love. Will you please give me the courage to say *no* and the wisdom to find my love in you? I know that your love for me isn't attached to my performance, and I really need to focus on your love right now."

If I've defined my motives (and they're pure and secure motives), and I'm still wrestling with the decision, I move to my third question.

3. What's the worst that could happen if I say *no*? This is an eye-opening question when I toss it out to people who've shared their tough situations with me. Most troubled youth workers will answer this by saying, "I could lose my job." I always respond the same way by saying,

"*Really?* That's the worst thing that could happen to you? My friend, that's not even close to the worst thing that could happen when compared with losing your family, losing your passion for God, losing your heart for people, or becoming a phony just going through the motions and trying to please everyone."

Here's the key to this question: The worst that can happen to you by saying *no* in any given situation is usually not bad enough to change your answer to *yes*. That is, if you've already defined *what matters most* to you. That's a key ingredient in the decision-making process. (If you haven't taken the time to answer that crucial question, please return to page 45 and spend some time with Avoiding a Personal Crash & Burn.)

If these three questions don't quickly come to mind and help you formulate a credible and carefully thought-out response when someone requests something of you, don't feel embarrassed to present some other options in the meantime, such as—

- "I need some time to think this through."
- "I'd like to check my calendar to see what's happening before I decide."
- "I'm too unsure right now to give you an answer; I need a little time to pray and talk about this with people who are close to me so they can help me make decisions related to time and priorities."

As I've written this little book, I've been asking God to use my words, ideas, and experiences as permission for my youth ministry friends to say *no*. I'm convinced that many of us need the confidence to know it's going to be okay to add *no* to our ministry vocabulary. So I want to chal-

lenge you to become comfortable with saying *no* when it impedes your pursuit of *what matters most.*

Many years ago a veteran pastor gave me the opposite advice. He gave me permission to be busy. He saw something in me that he liked, and he wanted to mark me as his young, driven apprentice. I'll never forget the staff meeting where our senior pastor explained that he was tired from all the work that he had been doing and was on the verge of exhaustion. As he poured out his heart, this older pastor whispered in my ear these words: "That's called 'ministry,' and he better get used to it." This rude comment displayed his "secret" to ministry "success," and because I didn't know any better, it influenced my choices and led to a lot of pain. He believed those called to ministry should say *yes* to everyone and everything. He lived and modeled a busy life. In fact, his favorite saying was,

"I can never slow down because the Devil never slows down."

His motto sounded empowering to this young youth worker's ears. I wanted to put on my spiritual armor and charge into battle, to keep running and never stop serving God with zeal and passion. Unfortunately I learned the hard way that I can't run all the time. While I was constantly running (being busy), I actually dropped my spiritual armor along the way, making me weak and more vulnerable to the Enemy.

The Devil never slows down? Oh well. The Devil isn't my role model.

Those of us in ministry can't continue to live at a breakneck pace. Our lives and ministries may have never been faster, but our souls—by our own admission—have never been drier. Busyness does not equal effectiveness.

I believe there are a lot of good people serving in ministry today who will wake up at the end of their lives and wish they'd opened up a big can of *NO* more often. But because they didn't, those things that mattered most didn't get the time and attention they needed.

Please don't allow that to happen to you! Please make the time to figure out what it will take for you to focus on *what matters most.* This book won't be useful to you until it becomes personal. In other words, you have to practice saying *no.* This may require some radical decisions on your part, but those decisions may keep your life from crashing. No one wins when a life is wrecked.

Before you put this book down, pause long enough to consider what your life and ministry could look like if you were deeply connected and intimate with God.

The fruitfulness from your life would be more abundant than you've ever imagined.

Your ministry would be more powerful than you've ever dreamed possible.

And all because you took a little time to—

1) Define *what matters most.*

2) Ask some tough questions of yourself.

3) Add *no* to your vocabulary.

I know you can do this, and I know it will help. Thanks for caring enough about your life, your church, and your spiritual legacy to begin feeling comfortable with and confident about saying *no* so you can start saying *yes* to *what matters most.*

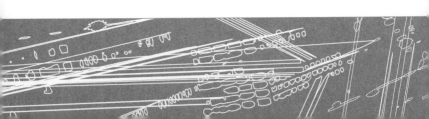